We Are Like Wells

We Are Like Wells

SAM MARACIC

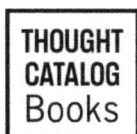

BROOKLYN, NY

THOUGHT
CATALOG
Books

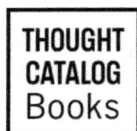

All rights reserved. Designed by KJ Parish. Cover photography by ©
Joel Filipe

Published by Thought Catalog Books, a division of The Thought &
Expression Co., Williamsburg, Brooklyn. Founded in 2010, Thought
Catalog is a website and imprint dedicated to your ideas and stories.
We publish fiction and non-fiction from emerging and established
writers across all genres. For general information and submissions:
manuscripts@thoughtcatalog.com.

First edition, 2017

ISBN: 978-1945796364

Printed and bound in the United States.

10 9 8 7 6 5 4 3 2 1

To my parents (all four of you) for consistently showing me what it means to be loved. You are the strongest, most selfless people I know, and I am forever grateful to call you mine.

To Danielle for understanding this journey unlike any other. You are more than my sister.

And to Mike, for being the best friend, confidant and rock a human could ever ask for.

CONTENTS

Introduction   1

Thoughts on Emotion, Growth, and What It Means to be Truly Human   3

Emotion as an Ingredient for Growth   7

The Strength Complex   11

5 Excuses You Need to Stop Making for Yourself   13

A Few of the Ways Anxious People Love   15

We Remain   17

How to Ruin Your Relationship in 5 Easy Steps   19

This is When We'll Lose the War   21

Be the One to Show Up   23

The Things People Who Practice Self-Love Do Differently   25

When Your Wanting Crumbles   29

Breathing in the Big   31

The Things I Would Tell my Teenage Self Today   33

Be Proud of Every Step You Take (Even the Tiny Ones)   37

Here is What I Realized   39

About the Author   41

Introduction

I once heard someone say that people are like wells because we vary in width and construction and depth. And though try as we may in times of struggle or stress, it is impossible to manufacture sameness.

Our expanses exist as what they are, and no one is responsible for the difference. Under this assumption, the degree to which we feel things (and also, perhaps the way we perceive them) has more to do with how we're assembled, and less to do with what we are perceiving.

If that is the case, and we are all just built of opposing depths and different degrees of filling, how do we find a healthy middle ground with the ones we love?

I for one am certainly not sure how the wells of our souls are constructed. Maybe the outer walls are the result of experience, or age or growth. And perhaps the material used is an extension of self—a definitive representation of something that will always be.

We may never know.

But I'd like to remain optimistic in my belief that somehow we do have control—if not over how we're built, then at least, over what we're filled with.

Maybe this notion is right. Perhaps I may never share the same depth as a friend, or a parent or a partner. Or maybe my expanse is wider rather than down-reaching. I do not know. But that's not what's important.

What is important is what's inside our wells. We make that decision. We can choose to be brimming with love and wonder and excitement, just as we can choose to be filled with regret or contention or hate.

At the end of the day, there is a place in this world for all shapes and sizes of people and souls and wells. Because really it's what inside that matters—that's what defines us all.

It is my hope that this book, a compilation of work written and toiled over throughout the course of many years, exists as a celebration of our human sameness. A springboard for contemplation, a genesis for growth and maybe, in some small way, a source of strength. Some of these words have made their way to the expanse that is the internet, while others have yet to be seen. All, however, have come from a place of personal learning, living and of course, struggling. I am innately grateful for those moments that have defined my experience thus far, and perhaps even more so, for the people that have helped me to navigate (though not always gracefully) the ups and downs native to life.

1

Thoughts on Emotion, Growth, and What It Means to be Truly Human

If someone were to ask you to describe the most important lesson you've learned from life thus far, how would you respond?

Because I'm not sure I could.

But that's not to say I haven't tried.

As an inherently anxious thinker, I cannot remember a time in which I wasn't instinctively reflective. Reflective upon whom I was, reflective upon what I wanted, reflective even upon circumstances I had no part in controlling. And to this day, I remain very much the same. At times my musings have rendered me fervent for experience and at others, apprehensive of feeling anything at all. I have been my own best friend and also, my own worst enemy. Most often, I stumble between both.

And yet despite my ever-evolving search for self-awareness, the metaphorical road on which I travel has never ceased to present new diversions. Bringing me back to questions I thought I had answered, and navigating me instead toward very different solutions.

At twenty-six years old I can wholeheartedly say I know very little for certain. So, it may come as no surprise that from where I stand, translating the idiosyncrasies of experience into life lessons still seems a bit premature. I'd like to instead believe that in the most organic way possible, my reflections have simply led me to thoughts—thoughts I have consistently revisited and arrived at, time and time again. They are by no means authoritative. However, today they are the closest I have come to a personal truth.

In order to find, you must be willing to look.

The "ah-ha" moments we seek to provide us with the answers to life's big questions rarely ever come to fruition, or at least not in the way we expect them to. Any truth worth finding requires work. It must be dug for, grappled with and pulled from deep below the surface. The truly exhausting beauty of exploration is that from it, we are better equipped to identify the most authentic, actualized parts of ourselves. We cannot do this if we are looking ahead or turning back. This can only be done in the here and now.

We are not our misgivings—but we are not our assets either.

Attachment to the opinions of others leaves us open for unsteadying. Praise as much as criticism has the power to shape and define self-perception. Surface judgments are unreliable at best. They prevent us from seeking a sense of stability that only lives within. Ultimately, we alone must be the marshals of our happiness.

Sometimes you need to simply be where you are.

The human experience ebbs and flows in a way that renders both the good and the bad equally important. Each and every one of us is entitled to operate within a moment of sadness, excitement, fear or anxiety—if that is where we are. Feeling our emotions fully is what enables us to better understand them, and in the greater sense, understand ourselves. However, in order to learn rather than linger, we must introduce purpose into the equation. Purposefully acknowledging where we are makes us each more attuned to what we need during life's inevitable chaos.

Vulnerability does not weakness make.

Exposing yourself bare and leaving your soul open to emotional damage is frightening. However, without change, we are incapable of growth. A lack of vulnerability is native only to those who wish to remain stagnant.

Emotion is not built for categorization.

To be truly human is to acknowledge that at times, parts of our condition are simply too tangled to unwind alone. Social conditioning has led many to believe their feelings must first be externally validated before seeking help in mediating them. All lives are confronted with shadows. Varying in the degree to which they present themselves perhaps, but always garnished with an absence of light. It is a far braver endeavor to move beyond those dark, dusty stumbling blocks than to toil under the guise that they simply don't exist. The guidance of others, be it professional or otherwise, can often empower our ability to do so.

When presented with the choice to be either a puddle or an ocean, I will forever seek to be the latter.

To truly live, one must experience. My feelings, emotions and anxieties are proof that I am not only living but also uncovering opportunities for growth and evolution along the way. When properly acknowledged our depth allows us to dismantle surface level systems that would have otherwise dictated a very shallow existence. So, while some may point out that puddles are less complicated, I would argue that they are certainly no better off for it.

2

Emotion as an Ingredient for Growth

By our very nature, we, as humans, are programmed to exist as impassioned creatures; creatures who ride through waves of emotions on a regular basis. Feelings of happiness are easy; they are the ones to which we look forward to with anticipation and the ones on which we affectionately reflect.

However, as each of us knows all too well, happiness isn't all that exists, and it's certainly not the culmination of a life's worth of experiences.

In a world where happiness (something that looks very different for each of us) remains the ultimate destination, what are we left to do with the not-so-sought-after feelings? (The ones we don't look forward to experiencing. The ones that bend and bruise us from the inside out.)

I've heard it said that motivation demands a prompt, something to propel us forward and keep us evolving. Well, if this is truly the case, then one could contend that there is no greater trigger than that of emotion.

Stimulation to expand ourselves is everywhere, but most often, I have found that it exists in the places we are least likely to look. The emotions that lie in the depths of life's ugly underbelly are the ones that force us to progress, and as much as they hurt, they are the ones from which we are meant to learn.

Fear

The sobering truth is that no man (or woman) is without fear.

However, recognizing the things that bring out our discomfort is, in actuality, the best way to overcome what it is that is holding us back.

We need fear to remind us of our humanness and to push us beyond the boundaries we create for ourselves. Fear is a powerful thing, and while it can be paralyzing, when conquered, there is no greater sense of liberation to be had.

There's a reason why bravery is valued: It is difficult. Like they say, "With great risk, comes great reward." Fear forces us to look risk square in the eye and throw it a metaphorical F-YOU. That is growth, and when everything is said and done, isn't that what life's all about?

Nothing worth having—a love, a friendship or even a career—is achieved without that leap of faith. It's not about forgetting what we fear, but rather, acting and progressing in spite of it.

Insecurity

There is no worse feeling than one that makes you question yourself. Regardless of the cause, to put it not-so-gently, insecurity is a bitch. Once we find the strength to move beyond the pain it provokes, the emotion of insecurity exists as an important reminder that we must truly value ourselves.

The faster we acknowledge and accept the fact that perfection does not exist, the faster we will be empowered to no longer chase it. Innately and honestly loving who you are is probably the hardest and ironically, most important gift you can give yourself.

Loneliness

The sense of "going at it" alone is one that I doubt anyone will truly get used to, and truthfully, I don't believe we should. Community is a massive part of who we are as human beings because ultimately, we need each other.

However, we also need to develop the capabilities necessary to stand on our own. This is why from time to time loneliness in all of its darkness can be a useful feeling. The soul knows what it needs, it's the physical self that isn't always willing to listen.

Our rawest emotions are as powerful as we allow them to be.[1]

1. Previously published by Elite Daily under the title "Three Unlikely Emotions that Spark Motivation and Positivity Within".

3

The Strength Complex

Somewhere along the winding road of human development, society veered off course. Our sense of navigation went awry, and amid a mix of disorientation and "progress" came the dangerous notion that strength should be solitary. That it should be defined by one's ability to act through adversity without the influence, aid or awareness of another. That at its very core, should exist only self.

I tend to disagree with that sentiment.

When we are born, we are born to face struggle. We learn to fall and to fumble, occasionally crawling our way from one point to the next. At times, the act of picking ourselves up extends far beyond discomfort. It tests and challenges us, demanding every ounce of strength we possess until finally, we return to a standing position. From these moments we hope to grow stronger and more capable than when we began—and usually we do.

But what about the times when we don't?

What about those dark, unspoken circumstances that render us utterly incapable of getting back up? What happens when try as we may, the climb just seems too steep?

Well, I'd like to think, that "we" happen.

"We" in the most collective sense of the word, steady the ground beneath one another, providing a gentle reminder of what it means to keep going.

Or at least, that's how it should be.

It seems to me that our innate need for human connectedness has been severely misinterpreted. Assistance isn't wholly synonymous with reliance, and yet, all too often it is presented that way. Like failure, growth exists as a powerful result of our humanity, but in every single sense, so does our impulse for empathy. Whether we physically can get up on our own or not isn't what's important, it's that in times of hardship, we shouldn't always have to.

Our world is filled with gray matter. It exists in the form of questions and hopefully once explored, transforms into something like discovery. So it is no wonder, that at times each and every one of us has struggled. Whether the result of an external environment, internal battle, illness or all of the above, no human should be made to feel like it isn't okay to ask for guidance while seeking what exists between the black and the white. When we limit one another from either soliciting or accepting help, we confine human lives to an unnatural place of stagnancy. We remain forever crawling, carrying our pain along with our battles and maybe most tragically, do so all in the midst of retreat.

And so, while the notion that "therapy" (in a strictly clinical sense) is for everyone may be false, the belief that we do not all require each other's aid in some capacity or another is not.

Strength isn't an act to be exclusively performed alone. It is to be transferred and cultivated among each and every one of us, until both the crawling sufferer and sound, helping hand, can walk in pace, side by side.

4

5 Excuses You Need to Stop Making for Yourself

1. Whatever you're grappling with in this moment is your permanent condition.

You are not your ailments or your afflictions. You are not the things you struggle to overcome or the things that slow you down from time to time. To put it bluntly, you deserve more than that. Even though this feels like forever, it isn't. Remember that fact and use it to help you find faith in the moments of weakness.

2. The way you see your world is, in fact, how it really exists.

If it's true that energy flows where attention goes then I guess you could say perception is key. As easy as it may feel to see the world around us with judgment and fear, we are certainly no better for it. When you're wandering around in the dark it's hard to find the light. Don't let anyone tell you otherwise. It can challenge every bit of your being, to say the least. However, that doesn't mean it isn't there. Reach out and find ways to continue the search. Find people that help to make that possible. And above all, remember that thoughts are only thoughts. You alone are the one that gives them power. Don't trust every little rumination that comes to mind, especially if it isn't one that serves you.

3. You will be happy when X, Y and Z finally come to fruition.

This is a slippery slope, one many of us are likely familiar with. After the high of achieving external things is over, we are forced once again to sit with ourselves. The only way to break this cycle is to purposefully slow down. To be still long enough to realize we already have everything we need. To put it frankly, you cannot fill yourself with "stuff," no matter how hard you try, or how often you succeed.

4. It's too embarrassing to reach out.

Give the people you love more credit. Trust that whatever you're experiencing, either good or bad, they want to share in with you. You are not alone. Your life, your success, your happiness, they all matter to someone. Just believe that, and let them in. Let people surprise you, and remember when it's your turn, to simply do the same.

5. You're not allowed to feel less than okay.

Life isn't a consistent mirage of rainbows and butterflies, and to believe otherwise is to feed into a false reality. Here me now when I say you are permitted to struggle with real pain or emotion. If you were not, well then you wouldn't be much of a human, would you?

Acknowledging that you aren't a robot doesn't mean you are giving up or conceding to a life any less wonderful than you hope for it to be. All it says is that you're working through shit, and that's noble. It's courageous, and it's real.

5

A Few of the Ways Anxious People Love

At first, they will love with anticipation. They will commit with a fear that the metaphorical "other shoe" may drop at any moment. This isn't to say they don't believe in you, or the bond you've built. It's simply a product of their nature, and sometimes, it may take awhile to kick.

They are thoughtful (sometimes to the point of overanalyzing). To put it simply, they care about everything in their lives with an incredibly deep sense of investment. They find joy in bringing their partner happiness but also inherently fear doing the opposite. As a result...

They may be liable to respond from a place of emotion, rather than logic. Remember that metaphorical shoe? In times of stress or disagreement, they tend to fear it is finally falling. The gravity of small situations can feel a lot larger when operating under the assumption that the worst case scenario is occurring. At times, this reaction may even result in a self-fulfilling prophecy leading to heightened tension and anxiety.

They deeply fear disappointing others, especially their partners. Innately hard on themselves, anxious thinkers are constantly on the lookout for ways they can do or be better. This can make feelings of security especially challenging to achieve. However, in some ways their concern also fuels their behavior, proving them to be some of the most loyal and dedicated partners.

They often require time to recharge. Anxious minds have a tendency to feel hectic, and at times, understandably tiresome (which is why the ability to disconnect for a night in or a few hours of alone time can be incredibly valuable). Constant socializing can leave them feeling especially depleted, and in need of respite. This isn't to say they don't enjoy time with their partner or family and friends, but rather crave some quiet to re-energize. Finding a person who is willing to join in on that time or respect their occasional need to reboot is everything.

They aren't afraid to put in the work. As human beings, each and every one of us has our own list of idiosyncrasies that inform who we are. Sure, when it comes to love there will always be room for improvement. However, in the grand scheme of offenses, I'd say concern is hardly the worst. While anxious minds may scrutinize conversations or have a propensity for overreacting (which when unaddressed can be a problem), they're also hyper-aware of the things that matter most. Their tendency to evaluate situations (though sometimes to their disadvantage) forces internal exploration. This analysis not only makes anxious people more self-aware (this includes both their strengths and their flaws) but also more sensitive and sympathetic toward those they love.

6

We Remain

We are all broken and battered and bruised,
perfectly imperfect and worn.

We battle the shadows,
push back against the hurt,
crawling our way toward the light.

But the fight that I've managed and the war that I've waged is one
that is solely my own.

I can't ask you to feel what I've felt.

I don't need you to see what I've seen.

Just be kind with the scars,
understand that they're there.
And know that I will try too.

Because whether they make you big—bigger than you thought you
were built,
or smaller than something to matter—
the blazes that you've doused, they are yours.
And all of that fight,
well, that is yours, too.

The look and the feel or our stories may be different,
but the fact that we're here—
that is not.

Standing between your demons and mine,
I can see what it means to survive.
I can see what it means to live on.

Some things in this life are performative.
They are not just meant for the experience.
They seek to be verbalized and felt.

Walking through the fire isn't always enough.
Acknowledging you did,
that's the key.

7

How to Ruin Your Relationship in 5 Easy Steps

1. Reject opportunities to say you're sorry.

Give weight only to your feelings, and dismiss the others along the way. Forget that just because you didn't think it or feel it or mean it, the situation is still worthy of your regard. Settle instead on silence or a passive suggestion to move on. Decline giving the other person what they're after (because it's not so much about the actual words as it is the effort behind them). Refuse to let the other person know they have been seen and accepted, even when not fully understood.

2. Think (mostly) about yourself.

Be passionate, but only about the things that hold weight in your universe. Your enjoyments, your fears, your problems. Forget entirely that there exists a plethora of experiences outside of your own. That each and every one of us is feeling and fearing and thinking meaningful things. Remain too caught up within your world to see what lies beyond that place.

3. Assume without question, that the people you love will always be around.

Reason with yourself that there will be another time. There will be plenty of nights together and endless opportunities to enjoy. Assure yourself you aren't operating within some kind of hour glass system. You've got your whole life, and so do they.

4. Forget to express gratitude.

Do not prioritize, and if you do, be wrongly selective about where your attention lies. Grow so accustomed to sweet actions and loving thoughts that you fail to recognize their importance altogether. Replace appreciation with assumption. Become so comfortable that you see each meaningful expression as mundane. Believe that love lies only in the grand gestures, rather than the simple moments that once defined your happiness.

5. Refuse to grow.

Remain stagnant. Feel so rooted in the place within which you reside that the idea of further growth feels unthinkable. Shy away from any desire to develop, to progress or to expand. Expect that those around you do the same. Do not root for their dreams or encourage their success, and do not support yours either. Instead, remain solely content where you are. Overlook your own ability to strive, the individual strength you have to bloom. Forget that you are fully whole, and have the power to constantly, repeatedly do great things.

8

This is When We'll Lose the War

This is when we'll lose the war

When we stop choosing love and hope and faith.
When we refuse to just simply say, "I'm sorry."
When we ignore the little signs and signals of distress.
When we give another voice to the anger.

We'll lose the war when we forget we're on the same side.

That we're fighting and bleeding for the same very thing—the thing
that once kept this together.

When we glorify our fight, our power and our words.

These are just battles—love and life and being human.
But every little battle, every fight and tattered moment—well they
start to add up.

They spiral and snowball into war.

And war, well that's not so simple to escape.

We lose when we're afraid to admit,
that one after another the battles aren't just so small.

They're lethal.

They're torture.

They're worse.

But love is tangible.
It's a living and breathing thing.

It is finite
and breakable
and raw.

Sometimes it faces death.
But that doesn't mean it can't be revived

Because there's a difference between wanting and keeping.

We can stamp out the ego, lay down the weapons and words.
Look out across those enemy lines
and finally not see one another.

We lose the war when we chose to.
When we no longer fight to keep.
When we commit to the battle over and over.

Blindly

Perpetually

We choose.

But we don't have to make that decision,
no one is forcing our hands.

We can take a step back.
We can leave this thing together.
We can open our eyes.

It's now or never.

9

Be the One to Show Up

Show up for the people you love.

Show up because life with a ghost or a memory or a halfway anything is not much of a life at all. Let them know you're there—even if only in the most broken and imperfectly human way possible.

Show up because love isn't a state of being or a destination or a much longer journey through life. Show up because love is an action and it requires a steady force of energy to exist.

Show up because love isn't stagnant—show up because neither are you.

Show up for the big stuff—celebrate and cry. Share in the experiences that will undoubtedly shape lives beyond your own.

Don't go through the motions, or pretend to feel what they feel. Feel what you feel, but try not to feel it alone.

Show up for the small moments, the ones we're conditioned to forget. The pajama filled nights, the long road trips home, the seconds and minutes and hours that have truly defined your love. Really, please promise to show up for those.

Show up for the "I'm sorry," the one we often just decide to overlook.

Never underestimate the power of that apology. Even if it's too short, or too late or unwanted and ill-received, show up for it anyway.

Show up for the hard conversations because life is built to be messy.

Be honest and brave.

Leave everything you feel on the table.

But if you can't do that—if you're not ready yet.

Well, then at least find a way to show up.

Show up to figure it out.

To learn and to lose.

To discover whatever the fuck your life is meant to be about.

Showing up isn't for forcing a feeling or a relationship or a dream, and it's not about clinging to what could or should be. It's about ending the avoidance. It's about accountability and being vulnerable. It's for putting in enough work to know who and what is worth fighting for. And it's for seeing with less hesitation—who and what is not.

Show up for yourself.

Give yourself a real shot, a true chance at whatever it is that your mind wanders toward right before you fall asleep.

Even when it feels hard and unnatural or incredibly frightening, show the fuck up—because it's the only great choice that you have: to be the one to show up.

10

The Things People Who Practice Self-Love Do Differently

If there is one topic that promises to elicit discussion, it is undoubtedly the topic of love. Either in search for or defense of, love has instigated people to face fears, suffer loss and even meet death in its name. And we hear it all the time—love of country, love of faith, love of family. But in the midst of daily life, there is one kind of love that seems to fall by the wayside. It is the kind that we often forget to talk about, and yet, also the very one that makes the others possible. It empowers, it sustains and it can be incredibly difficult to acquire.

If you haven't figured it out yet, I'm talking about self-love.

To say you exercise self-love is easier said than done. True self-love requires a willingness to remain open about both the good and the bad parts of who you are, and to face that dichotomy, very honestly, each and every day.

Here are the things people who practice self-love do differently.

They honor every phase of their lives since each has provided space for growth.

When we find the courage to embrace every experience with equal parts objectivity and compassion, it becomes far less daunting to alter the spaces they occupy within our minds. And though it may remain a challenge at times, people who practice self-love recognize even the most cringe-worthy experiences as building blocks for development. Liberating oneself from things that may have once provoked sadness or shame, enable a clearer sense of awareness and disarm the dissenting words or opinions of others.

They understand that when something stops creating joy, it is time to stop pursuing it.

Whether it be through time spent alone or past experience, they have come to learn that no opportunity is worth compromising your happiness for.

They respect the necessity of quality versus quantity.

In freeing themselves from the fallacy that friendship is defined by the number of companions you possess, they can more deeply recognize the importance of time and where it is invested. Rather than seeking or sustaining surface level interactions for the external gratification they provide, people who practice self-love nurture the relationships that build them up.

They give themselves space to cultivate and connect with their passions.

Whether it's going to the gym, traveling or simply reading a book, they actively pursue interests and give themselves time to explore them. They understand the necessity of personal expansion and remember to dedicate energy toward the things they enjoy.

The opinions of other people do not define their perception of self.

They appreciate and respect the perspectives of others, especially those whom they love. However, they have reconciled it with themselves so that both praise and criticism remain of the same value within their psyche. Opinions exist, but they do not characterize one way or another.

They are not only willing to admit to their misgivings, but also forgive themselves for them.

They of all people know how truly imperfect they are. However, most days, they have given up on beating themselves down. They look at themselves the way they would look at a friend, with compassion and acceptance. Above all, they value the importance of understanding and know that some lessons can only be learned through falling down.

They welcome their feelings as they come.

In their eyes, running from emotion feels counterintuitive. They recognize their feelings as indicators of something deeper and use them to better navigate discomfort, contentment and everything in between.

They are okay with spending time alone.

Although the companionship of friends and family is something we all need, it is not meant to be had twenty-four seven. As human beings, we require space for personal time and reflection. So, whether it has been a natural tendency or something they've had to work toward, these are the individuals that have come to find comfort in simply sitting with themselves. They understand that the impulse for constant, external stimulation is one that must be remedied from within, and they are not afraid to explore that experience.

They listen to themselves.

Mind, body and spirit—they are acutely in tune with their needs. Whether it's simply more sleep or an entirely new career path, they trust that voice in their heads, and actively seek to balance every facet of who they are.

They understand that while external love (be it familial, romantic

or platonic) is irreplaceable, the most important relationship they will ever have is with themselves.

They have retired from misplacing the responsibility of their happiness on the shoulders of others. It is simply too important. Instead, they take solace in the friendship they maintain with themselves, and in doing so use it to bolster the other relationships in their lives. Ultimately they've learned that contentment begins and ends with you.

11

When Your Wanting Crumbles

Look around you. Look hard, but never deep. Let the scrutiny burn and the examination exhaust as it moves from pupil to pupil.

See what they are doing, having, enjoying. Glorify the image of that distant ivory tower, floating above the little space in which you occupy. Crave it from below. Yearn for that platform in all of its elevated authority.

Keep your eyes above the surface as you watch, just enough to admire from afar—the life, the dream, the fantasy.

But don't look below. No—never, never underneath.
Remember how close to the ground you are in comparison. Remember the uncertainty, the want, the need, the deficiency—the absence that exists in looking up beyond yourself.

Imagine what it would be like if you were more like them.
Lighter, brighter, higher.

If only.

Let their "haves" build—cultivating so many worlds within your mind. Run through them like a maze. Wondering all the while, which if any, could be yours.

Whose would you want?

How would you choose?

Test them.

Try them on for size, for fit. Climb the stairs, preparing to transcend once and for all in someone else's mast.

Enter their space, only to find a rush of cold blanket your form.

Your eyes can no longer circumvent what is there. You see so much more than you expected. Cracks and stains, tatters and breaks. Your elevation doesn't seem so high from in here. This space is so much smaller than you imagined.

Where is all of the light you thought you saw?
Where is the grand perfection?
The warmth?

Withdraw.

Continue moving, from tower to tower, watching them crumble away in the wake of disillusion.

There is nothing behind but rubble and soot.
Eventually, all that's left is you.

Your mind.

Your tower.

Walk inside, recognizing the smell, the look, the feel.
It's not as cold as you remembered, certainly not like some of the others.

The cracks really aren't so bad.

And the breaks you have, well maybe they are fixable.
They must be.

After all, nothing else has been what it's seemed.

12

Breathing in the Big

I used to believe my insides were built too big. That beneath my small frame of humanity lies a depth too tremendous in size, too weighted with intensity.

I felt too much. I was too much to love. I was on overload, my nerves maxed out with fear because there was too much in me for one body to hold. Surely not everyone is like this. Surely I am the only one. Nobody talks about feeling too much for their lives; too big for their bodies. I thought it was me.

So I used to believe I needed to change this. I needed to shrink that which made me so expansive. Dial it down. Rein it in. Dilute. Replace what was with only what should be.

This looked like suppressing how I felt. How hungry I was. What I did, how I reacted, what I thought, what I said, who I loved. Everything was calculated and decided upon. I was a caricature of a person I never even wanted to be. A character I was writing in my mind. I therapied and apologized. Self-hated and subdued. Ran and cried and pushed it below.

Pushing, until it bubbled.

Flowing over the rims of my cage, taking up residence where it was always meant to lie. Tired and exhausted. I let my truth envelop me. I fell beneath its surface, immersed in all of the bigness I was not meant to be. My thoughts. My emotions. My fears. My self.

I did what I was afraid to do. I thought I was breaking, giving up, letting myself go under.

But I did not drown. I did not gasp or fumble or hurt.

I breathed. Deeply.

I was free.

Finally.

13

The Things I Would Tell my Teenage Self Today

1. Not having all of the answers is simply part of the process. It is your right as a kid—and a human—not to know. Revel in where you are now, and look toward the future knowing that the universe has a far greater plan for you than you can ever create for yourself.

2. You are meant to make mistakes, but you are also meant to learn from them.

3. Trusting your instincts is necessary. So, feel good about having the strength to say "yes" or "no."

4. Accepting that you will not always fit in is the most liberating and telling reality, one that will better prepare you to understand the importance of true belonging.

5. No book, relationship, achievement or outfit will teach you who you are, but there is something to be gained from every aspect of life you explore.

6. Education (whether it be through conventional means or other-wise) does matter, and in the real world people will care about what you add to a conversation. So embrace every opportunity you have to learn.

7. Sometimes showing vulnerability is the bravest thing you can do.

8. The walls you create will protect, but they will also fortify. Letting others in is a frightening thing. It will lead to moments of heartache and periods of disappointment; do it anyway. The human experience is meant to be shared.

9. Be good to people, even when you feel you have no reason to be. (Hint: There is always a reason to be.)

10. Boys will come and go. You'll be okay.

11. There is no clear destination. As humans, we are constantly evolving, and to pigeonhole yourself to the person you are now is only to inhibit progress necessary for growth. Accept that who you are today is not who you will be tomorrow.

12. Have the compassion to do the same for others.

13. Even on the darkest of days, good does exist. It is your job to look beyond the fog in search of it.

14. "Mean girls" (and boys, for that matter) exist beyond middle school, and unfortunately, that may never change. Send them as much love as you can. They are usually the ones who need it most.

15. Often times, the pain caused by a first love, loss or traumatic life event is out of your control. Allowing your pain to dictate the way you see others and the way you see the world is not. As hard as it may seem, do not let those negative experiences determine your perspective.

16. Live for yourself. Explore the things that make you happy, even if they are not considered cool or significant by someone else's standards.

17. Try at everything, even if you're terrible. In the end, you'll either be proud of yourself for not giving up or less terrible than when you began. Effort is and will always be attractive.

18. Much of what you will take from life depends simply on your choice to show up. Being present and in the moment may be one of the greatest challenges, but it also promises the most honest rewards.

19. To appreciate the beauty of others, you must first be willing to do the same with yourself.

20. Strangely enough, the adults are right, stop rushing to grow up. Enjoy your youth. Have fun being a kid, and hang on to that irreplaceable innocence until you are truly ready to let it go.

21. The people you love won't be around forever. Be grateful for every family event you've had the opportunity to attend.

22. Comparing yourself to others will get you nowhere.

23. Even when you feel like the world is against you, it's not.

24. Say thank you to your parents, they're doing the best they know how to.

25. Everything comes full circle eventually. It is your job to simply be the best human you can be.

14

Be Proud of Every Step You Take (Even the Tiny Ones)

Be proud that you're making steps, even if small, toward your dreams.

Be proud that you're working—taking action in the direction of something bigger than yourself. Something that will at some point, even if not today or tomorrow, bring you closer to where you're meant to be.

Have faith in your ability to plan. Maybe not thoroughly quite yet, but to aim and operate nonetheless.

Be proud that you're not without fear. That at times you are frightened and confused. And yet despite the uncertainty in yourself, you're maneuvering anyway. You're facing the doubt head on.

Know that you are making progress.

With every cent saved and lesson learned, you are becoming a better version of yourself.

Be proud that you are rallying for your future.

That success hasn't simply happened overnight.

That you can appreciate the journey for what it is: an adventure.

Be proud that you're caring for yourself. Moving, cooking a meal, reading a book. Appreciate that simple ability to support your own needs. Perhaps it feels silly or insignificant, but it is proof that you are more fortunate than most.

Be proud of the trust you have placed in this process. Your gratitude for what is and your optimism for what may be: herein lies your power. It is a reminder that perspective is everything. Be proud to have acquired that wisdom.

Find satisfaction in all that you have done, even if you feel like you're just getting started. You've made it this far, and that's something.

Be proud you've chosen to take the road less traveled. Be proud of your innate desire to want more. Have gratitude for the people that surround you. For the ones who lift you up and hold your hand, for the people who bring light to your journey.

But also find thanks for the ones who don't. For the doubters, the naysayers and the nonbelievers, they've made you a different kind of strong. Resilient, resolute and pliable. You are you because of them, as well.

Never forget that you matter. Your effort, your loyalty, your commitment. Be proud because those are the attributes that hold weight.

Find faith in the failures, the slow starts and the bumps in the road. They aren't hindering your greatness, they are creating it.

15

Here is What I Realized

Quiet is hard to come by or at least, it is for me. Even in the calmest of moments, the earliest of mornings, the chatter has never been far. Listening to my thoughts, it's as if it's second nature, as routine and commonplace as a scar. It's always there, to some degree.

It's hard to find quiet on the inside—to surrender the mind and silence the thoughts.

It's hard to build peace in that place. But in those faint moments, the ones that slip between feeling and theory, something incredible happens. Even if just momentarily, I muster the ability to go still.

Here, I recognize that I've been searching. Foraging to no avail for someone who will show me the answer. Perhaps it's not a person maybe it's a thing or a place, anywhere outside of this mind. An all-knowing guide to reveal which way is up. To teach me what it means to be me.

And isn't that ironic? And insane? To think that something outside of "me" could show me what it means to be me?

I guess what I hadn't seemed to realize (until this very moment) is that perhaps each of us already has those things. The things we can't seem to identify about ourselves. The things we keep fruitlessly seeking.

This brief pause in the clamor is what heals us. It is profound even despite its mundane presence. It is what links us back to those parts of ourselves. It isn't about spirituality or religion or some innately existential way of thinking. We discover what we need simply by existing, without judgment or opinion, just actively "being."

Soberingly aware in the silence of ourselves, this is where we hear.

About the Author

Sam Maracic is a writer and yoga teacher living and working in New York.

She is a graduate of St. Joseph's College, where she received her B.A. in Human Relations and Political Science with Minors in English and American Studies. Most recently, she received her Master's Degree in English from St. John's University.

YOU MIGHT ALSO LIKE:

101 Essays That Will Change The Way You Think by Brianna Wiest

You Are Enough by Becca Martin

Seeds Planted in Concrete by Bianca Sparacino

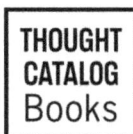

THOUGHT
CATALOG
Books

THOUGHT CATALOG

IT'S A WEBSITE.

www.thoughtcatalog.com

SOCIAL

facebook.com/thoughtcatalog
twitter.com/thoughtcatalog
tumblr.com/thoughtcatalog
instagram.com/thoughtcatalog

CORPORATE

www.thought.is